Main-Dish Soups

Little Vegetarian Feasts

MaiN-Dish Soups

Martha Rose Shulman

Illustrated by Debbie Drechsler
Designed by B. W. Honeycutt
Produced by The Miller Press, Inc.

Bantam Books

NEW YORK · TORONTO · LONDON · SYDNEY · AUCKLAND

Little Vegetarian Feasts
Main-Dish Soups
A Bantam Book/September 1992

Library of Congress Cataloging-in-Publication Data

Shulman, Martha Rose.
Little vegetarian feasts. Main-dish soups/Martha Rose Shulman;
illustrations by Debbie Drechsler; designed by B.W. Honeycutt;
produced by The Miller Press, Inc.

p. cm.
ISBN 0-553-08641-3
1. Soups. 2. Vegetarian Cookery. I. Title
TX757.S48   1992

641.8′13—dc20

92-834
CIP

Published simultaneously in the United States and Canada

**Bantam Books are published by Bantam Books, a division of Bantam
Doubleday Dell Publishing Group, Inc. Its trademark, consisting of the
words "Bantam Books" and the portrayal of a rooster, is Registered in
U.S. Patent and Trademark Office and in other countries. Marca Registrada.
Bantam Books, 666 Fifth Avenue, New York, New York 10103.**

Printed in THE UNITED STATES OF AMERICA
0 9 8 7 6 5 4 3 2 1

Main-Dish
Soups

Contents

IntRoducTioN

Soup is not only beautiful; it's also a satisfying supper, be it a thick, lusty potage or a lighter, more subtle and refined dish.

I don't agonize over my soups. Inspired by a few French women who are great cooks and never spend much time making dinner, I have learned that good soups can be blissfully uncomplicated, often as simple a combination as vegetables, water, herbs, and salt. A good stock will definitely contribute to a high-quality soup, but every soup in this book has been tested using only water, and they were all delicious.

You can make a meal out of almost any soup, because most of them are filling, even if they're light. That's why they're so perfect as an evening meal. The soups in this collection qualify as main dishes because they all contain a certain amount of at least one high-protein ingredient.

Soups make great dishes for entertaining, because many can be made in advance, at least up to a certain point. So whether it's just for you and the family or for family and friends, slice up a good loaf of bread, open a bottle of wine, and serve dinner in a bowl.

Soup Basics

Sautéing Vegetables in a Minimum of Fat: Use as little oil as you can get away with. To prevent the vegetables from burning, keep the heat very low, and use heavy-bottomed pots. Stir often. If the vegetables do begin to stick to the bottom of the pot, add a tablespoon or two of water and continue to cook over low heat, stirring often, until the vegetables are soft and fragrant.

Thickening Soups: Potatoes are the heroes here. Throw a couple of potatoes into vegetable soups, and they act as the thickener for the purees. Potatoes add body and flavor without overpowering the other vegetables in the soup, as well as lots of nutrients. A handful of rice thrown into a simmering broth will also serve to thicken a puree. When soups contain beans, the beans act as a natural thickener because of their starch. Even when you don't want a puree, you can blend a portion of the beans, say a cupful, and stir them back into the soup to give the broth more substance.

Blender vs. Food Mill vs. Food Processor: Whether you are pureeing part or all of your soup, you will get a completely different texture with each of these tools. A blender is most effective for a totally smooth soup, a food mill fitted with the medium blade for a thick soup that still has texture. Food processors puree unevenly, which is all right if a recipe instructs you to puree coarsely all or part of a soup (such as a bean soup), but not so good for smooth soups. They should never be used for potato soups, however, because the blade cuts too fast, causing the potatoes to become gummy. A blender—particularly the new portable blenders you can use right in the soup pot—works better because the blade is smaller. Always puree soups in batches and increase the speed gradually. Be careful; hot soup splashing outside the container can be dangerous.

Hearty Bean Soups

White Bean and Tomato Soup

Serves 6

A colorful, savory, garlicky meal, this can be made with fresh tomatoes in summer and canned tomatoes in winter.

1 tablespoon olive oil
1 large onion, chopped
4 to 6 large garlic cloves to taste, minced or
    put through a press
1 pound (2¼ cups) dried white beans,
    picked over and soaked overnight or for 6 hours
2 quarts water
a bouquet garni (page 26)
1 Parmesan cheese rind
2 teaspoons salt (or more to taste)
1½ pounds canned or fresh tomatoes,
    peeled, seeded, and chopped (about 2¼ cups)
½ teaspoon dried thyme *or* 1 teaspoon
    chopped fresh (or more to taste)
½ teaspoon dried oregano *or* 1 teaspoon
    chopped fresh (or more to taste)
freshly ground pepper to taste
6 tablespoons chopped fresh basil or parsley
2 ounces Parmesan cheese, grated (½ cup)

1. Heat the oil over low heat in a heavy-bottomed soup pot and add the onion and two of the garlic cloves. Cook, stirring, until the onion is soft and fragrant.

2. Drain the soaked beans and add them, along with the water, bouquet garni, and cheese rind. Bring to a boil, reduce heat, cover, and cook for 1 to 1½ hours, until the beans are just about tender. Remove a heaped cup of →

beans and puree in a blender or food processor. Stir back into the pot.

3. Add the remaining garlic, salt, tomatoes, thyme, and oregano and simmer for another 30 minutes or until the beans are thoroughly tender and the broth is fragrant. Add lots of freshly ground pepper, taste for salt, and stir in the fresh basil or parsley. Remove the Parmesan rind and the bouquet garni.

4. Serve, topping each portion with freshly grated Parmesan cheese.

PARMESAN RINDS

Whenever you buy a chunk of Parmesan, you're paying partly for the hard outer rind. Don't throw it out! The rinds give broth a marvelous, cheesy, Italian-style fragrance, with no addition of fat. One or two hard rinds from a piece of Parmesan cheese can be added directly to the broth or wrapped in cheesecloth along with the bouquet garni and added to the broth, then removed at the end of cooking. They're especially good in bean and vegetable soups.

Fragrant Bean and Pasta Soup

**This hearty Italian soup reminds me of minestrone, but
with fewer vegetables.**

2 tablespoons olive oil
1 large *or* 2 medium-size onions, chopped
4 to 6 large garlic cloves to taste, minced or
   put through a press
1 small carrot, chopped
1 celery rib, chopped
1 pound (2¼ cups) dried white, cranberry,
   kidney, or pinto beans, washed, picked
   over, and soaked overnight or for 6 hours
1 28-ounce can Italian-style tomatoes, with
   juice, chopped
2 quarts water
a bouquet garni (page 26)
1 or 2 Parmesan cheese rinds to taste
1 teaspoon dried oregano (2 teaspoons
   chopped fresh)
1 teaspoon dried thyme (2 teaspoons fresh leaves)
2 teaspoons salt, plus more to taste
freshly ground pepper to taste
¼ pound (about 1½ cups) penne, fusilli, or
   macaroni
3 ounces Parmesan cheese, grated (¾ cup)
½ cup chopped fresh parsley

1. Heat the oil over low heat in a large, heavy-bottomed
soup pot and add the onion, one garlic clove, the carrot,
and the celery. Stir together, cover partially, and sweat for →

five to 10 minutes, stirring often, until the vegetables are tender and fragrant.

2. Add the beans, tomatoes and their juice, another garlic clove, the water, bouquet garni, and Parmesan rinds. Bring to a boil, reduce the heat, cover and simmer for an hour.

3. Add the oregano, thyme, two teaspoons salt, and the remaining two to four garlic cloves (to taste). Cover and continue to simmer for another 30 to 60 minutes, until the beans are tender but not mushy. Remove the Parmesan rind and bouquet garni. Puree one cup of the beans in a blender or through the medium blade of a food mill and stir back into the soup. Add lots of freshly ground pepper and adjust the salt and garlic.

4. Bring the soup back to a boil and add the pasta. Cook al dente, about 10 minutes. Stir in ⅓ cup of the Parmesan and the parsley and serve, passing the remaining Parmesan at the table.

Note: If you are not serving the soup right away, don't add the pasta until shortly before serving, or it will soak up too much broth and become too soggy.

If you wish to add green vegetables, add them to the simmering broth about 15 minutes before serving or steam them separately and heat through in the soup just before serving.

Lentil and Swiss Chard Potage with Goat Cheese

Serves 6

Lentils and greens of all kinds always make a good match. If you want a thinner soup, reduce the amount of lentils by ½ cup. The soup will still be substantial.

1 pound Swiss chard
1 tablespoon olive oil
1 medium-size onion, chopped
4 large garlic cloves, minced or put through
  a press
1 pound (2 cups) lentils, washed
2 quarts water
a bouquet garni (page 26)
1 Parmesan cheese rind
salt and freshly ground pepper to taste
3 ounces not-too-salty fresh goat cheese
¼ cup chopped fresh parsley (or more to taste)
6 tablespoons plain low-fat yogurt or
  fromage blanc (page 58)
diced roasted red bell peppers for garnish
  (optional)

1. Cut the chard leaves away from the stalks, chop, and set aside. Slice the stalks.

2. Heat the oil over low heat in a heavy-bottomed soup pot and add the onion, the chard stalks, and half the garlic. Sauté until the onion is tender. Add the lentils, water, bouquet garni, and Parmesan rind. Bring to a boil, reduce →

heat, cover, and simmer for 40 minutes or until the lentils are tender. Stir in the remaining garlic, one teaspoon salt (or more to taste), and lots of freshly ground pepper.

3. Discard the bouquet garni and the Parmesan rind. Puree a cup of the lentils in a blender or food processor and stir back into the soup. Add the chopped chard leaves, cover, and simmer for another 5 to 10 minutes. Stir in the goat cheese and parsley, heat through until the cheese melts, adjust the seasonings, and serve, topping each bowl with a dollop of yogurt or *fromage blanc* and a spoonful of diced roasted red bell peppers if desired.

Brazilian Black Bean Soup

**How can so few ingredients yield such depth? Loosely
based on a recipe for the very meaty Brazilian *feijoada*,
this filling soup gets its special tangy flavor from
the oranges.**

> 1 tablespoon sunflower or olive oil
> 1 large *or* 2 medium-size onions, chopped
> 2 celery ribs, with leaves, chopped
> 4 to 6 large garlic cloves to taste, minced or
>   put through a press
> 1 pound (2¼ cups) dried black beans,
>   washed, picked over and soaked overnight
>   or for 6 hours
> 2 oranges, cut in half
> 9 cups water or vegetable stock (page 53)
> 1 bay leaf
> about 2 teaspoons salt
> freshly ground pepper to taste
> *fromage blanc* (page 58) or plain low-fat
>   yogurt plus chopped fresh chives, for garnish

1. Heat the oil in a heavy-bottomed soup pot and add the onion, celery, and one garlic clove. Sauté over medium-low heat until the onion is tender. Add the beans, oranges, two garlic cloves, the water or stock, and the bay leaf. Bring to a boil, reduce the heat, and simmer for one hour.

2. Add the salt and remaining garlic and continue to simmer, covered, for another hour or until the beans are tender. Remove the bay leaf and oranges and puree the soup →

coarsely in a blender, in a food processor, or through the medium blade of a food mill. Return it to the pot. Add lots of pepper, adjust the seasonings (add a little more salt or garlic if you wish), heat through, and serve, garnishing each bowl with a generous dollop of *fromage blanc* or yogurt and a sprinkling of chives.

Pureed Chick-Pea Soup with Fresh Mint

Serves 6

Fresh mint adds an exciting twist to this lemony, nourishing soup. Make it a day ahead for the best flavor.

1 pound (2¼ cups) dried chick-peas, picked over and soaked overnight or for 6 hours
1 medium-size onion, chopped
4 to 6 large garlic cloves to taste, minced or put through a press
9 cups water
a bouquet garni (page 26)
2 teaspoons salt (or more to taste)
freshly ground pepper to taste
juice of 1 large lemon (4 to 5 tablespoons or more to taste)
1 cup plain low-fat yogurt
6 tablespoons chopped fresh mint
1 tablespoon crushed cumin seeds (optional)

1. Drain the chick-peas and combine them with the onion, two cloves of the garlic, the water, and the bouquet garni in a large, heavy-bottomed soup pot. Bring to a boil, reduce the heat, cover, and simmer for one to two hours, until the beans are tender. Add the salt and remaining garlic, and simmer for about 15 minutes more. Remove the bouquet garni.

2. Puree the soup in a blender, in a food processor, or through the medium blade of a food mill and return it to the pot. Add pepper, heat through, and stir in the lemon juice and yogurt (if the soup seems too thick, add a little more yogurt or water). Taste and adjust the seasonings, adding more salt, garlic, or lemon juice as desired.

3. Serve, topping each bowl with a generous sprinkling of fresh mint leaves and a sprinkling of crushed cumin seeds and lemon juice if desired.

Note: This soup can also be served cold.

Black-eyed Pea Soup with Cilantro and Cumin

Serves 4

The cumin, garlic, and cilantro give this Mexican-style soup a zesty flavor. Don't forget the garnishes; this earthy soup needs their bright color.

1 tablespoon sunflower or olive oil
1 medium-size onion, chopped
3 to 4 large garlic cloves to taste, minced or put through a press
1 pound (2¼ cups) dried black-eyed peas, washed and picked over
9 cups water or vegetable stock (page 53)
1 bay leaf
1 to 2 teaspoons salt to taste
1 teaspoon ground cumin (or more to taste)
1 tablespoon red wine vinegar
leaves from 1 bunch of cilantro, chopped
freshly ground pepper to taste
fromage blanc (page 58) or plain low-fat yogurt and diced roasted red peppers for garnish

1. Heat the oil in a heavy-bottomed soup pot and add the onion and one garlic clove. Sauté over medium-low heat until the onion is tender. Add the peas, another clove of garlic, the water or stock, and the bay leaf. Bring to a boil, reduce the heat, cover and simmer for 30 minutes.

2. Add the salt, another two garlic cloves, cumin, vinegar, and half the cilantro. Continue to simmer, covered, for another 15 to 30 minutes, until the beans are tender but not mushy. Remove the bay leaf and puree two cups of the beans in a blender or food processor or through the medium blade of a food mill. Stir the puree back into the soup. Add lots of pepper, adjust the seasonings (add a little more salt or garlic if you wish), heat through, stir in most of the cilantro, and serve, garnishing each bowl with a dollop of *fromage blanc* or yogurt, a spoonful of diced roasted red peppers, and a sprinkling of chopped cilantro.

Lighter Vegetable Soups

Provençal Spinach and Potato Soup

Pour yourself a glass of chilled rosé or warming Côtes-du-Rhône, make a fire in the fireplace, and put together this soothing Provençal soup. It's loaded with spinach, which keeps all of its vitality because it simmers just long enough to set the eggs.

> 6 cups water, vegetable stock (page 53), or garlic broth (page 55)
> 5 large garlic cloves, minced or put through a press
> 1 tablespoon olive oil
> 1 pound (4 medium-size) new or russet potatoes, scrubbed and sliced
> a bouquet garni (page 26)
> ½ teaspoon dried thyme or sage *or* 2 teaspoons chopped fresh leaves
> salt to taste
> 2 pounds spinach, stems removed and leaves washed and chopped
> freshly ground pepper to taste
> 4 medium-size eggs
> 4 thick slices French bread or crusty whole wheat bread, toasted and rubbed with a cut clove of garlic

1. Combine the water or stock, garlic, olive oil, potatoes, bouquet garni, herbs, and salt to taste in a wide, heavy-bottomed soup pot or casserole. Bring to a boil, reduce →

the heat, cover, and simmer for 30 minutes. Remove the bouquet garni.

2. Stir in the spinach and freshly ground pepper, taste, and adjust the seasonings. Reduce the heat to a bare simmer.

3. Carefully break the eggs into the soup. As soon as they are set—after about six to eight minutes (or maybe a little longer; use your eyes)—bring the soup to the table and serve. Place a thick garlic crouton in each bowl and carefully ladle the soup, with an egg, on top.

Potato-Cheese Soup with Cumin or Caraway

Serves 6

Cumin or caraway jazzes up this well-known potato-cheese combo. Both spices work well, but you might like one better than the other.

1 tablespoon olive oil
4 medium-size leeks, white part only,
   cleaned and sliced
2 garlic cloves, minced or put through a press
1 tablespoon cumin seeds or caraway seeds,
   slightly crushed
2 pounds (8 medium-size) new or russet
   potatoes, scrubbed and diced
6 cups vegetable stock (page 53), garlic
   broth (page 55), or water
a bouquet garni (page 26)
salt to taste
2 cups low-fat milk
freshly ground pepper to taste
¼ pound Gruyère cheese, grated (1 cup)
1½ ounces Parmesan cheese, grated (⅓ cup)
chopped fresh parsley for garnish

1. Heat the oil over low heat in a heavy-bottomed soup pot and add the leeks. Cover partially and cook over low heat for five minutes, stirring often. Add the garlic and cumin or caraway and cook, stirring, for another couple of minutes. →

2. Add the potatoes, stock or water, bouquet garni, and salt and bring to a boil. Reduce the heat, cover, and simmer for 40 minutes or until the potatoes are very tender and the broth is fragrant. Remove the bouquet garni. Mash some of the potatoes against the side of the soup pot with the back of a wooden spoon or with a masher to thicken the soup.
3. Stir in the milk, add pepper, and heat through for 10 minutes. Add the cheeses, stir to melt, taste, and adjust the seasonings. Serve, garnishing each bowl with a sprinkling of chopped fresh parsley.

BOUQUET GARNI

A bouquet garni is a bundle of herbs and aromatics that is added to the simmering broth and discarded at the end of cooking. It always consists of a bay leaf, a few sprigs of thyme, and a sprig or two of parsley. Beyond that it can include an outer layer of a leek (which can serve as a wrapper for the other herbs), a rib or the leaves from a rib of celery, or a piece of fennel. The ingredients are tied together with kitchen string and added to the soup with the liquid ingredients.

Puree of Winter Vegetable Soup

Of course you could also make this thick, savory soup in spring, summer, or fall. Use a food mill rather than a blender so that you get a puree with some texture.

6 medium-size leeks, white part only, cleaned and sliced
1 small onion, chopped
1 to 2 garlic cloves to taste, minced or put through a press
2 medium-size carrots, chopped
1 celery rib, chopped
2 small turnips, peeled and chopped
2 pounds (8 medium-size) new or russet potatoes, scrubbed and diced
1 large Swiss chard stalk, washed and chopped
6 cups vegetable stock (page 53), intense mushroom broth (page 56), or water
a bouquet garni (opposite page)
salt and freshly ground pepper to taste
2 to 4 tablespoons dry white wine or sherry to taste
1 cup low-fat milk
1 cup plain low-fat yogurt or *fromage blanc* (page 58)
chopped fresh parsley for garnish

1. Combine the vegetables, stock, bouquet garni, and salt →

in a large, heavy-bottomed soup pot and bring to a boil. Reduce the heat, cover, and simmer for 45 minutes to an hour. **2.** Remove the bouquet garni and puree the soup through the medium blade of a food mill. Return the soup to the pot and stir in lots of freshly ground pepper and the wine or sherry. Adjust salt. Thin out as desired with milk. Heat through and serve, garnishing each bowl with a dollop of yogurt or *fromage blanc* and a generous sprinkling of chopped fresh parsley.

Chinese Cabbage and Tofu Soup

Serves 6

The mystery here is how a soup so healthful and quick to make can taste so good.

> 2 quarts vegetable stock (page 53), ginger-vegetable stock (page 54) or quick tamari-bouillon (page 54)
>
> 1 pound (½ medium-size head) Chinese or Savoy cabbage, shredded
>
> 6 scallions, both white and green parts, thinly sliced
>
> 1 garlic clove, minced or put through a press (optional)
>
> 2 to 3 tablespoons tamari soy sauce (to taste; omit if using quick tamari-bouillon)
>
> 2 tablespoons dry sherry
>
> 2 teaspoons grated fresh ginger
>
> ½ pound firm tofu, cut into thin slivers
>
> 1 tablespoon cornstarch, dissolved in 2 tablespoons water
>
> 2 medium-size eggs, beaten
>
> salt and freshly ground pepper to taste
>
> 6 tablespoons chopped cilantro for garnish

1. Combine the stock, cabbage, scallions, garlic if desired, tamari, sherry, ginger, and tofu in a large soup pot and bring to a boil. Reduce the heat and simmer for 10 minutes. The cabbage should be cooked through but still retain some texture. Stir in the dissolved cornstarch and stir the soup until slightly thickened.

2. Beat the eggs in a bowl and slowly stir them into the →

soup, using a fork or chopstick to thread the eggs through the simmering soup so that they form little strands. Add freshly ground pepper, taste the soup, and salt if desired.

3. Serve at once, garnishing each bowl with cilantro.

Sweet and Spicy Red Cabbage and Apple Soup

Serves 4 to 6

Sweet, spicy, and easy, this makes a perfect dinner on a cold winter night.

1 tablespoon sunflower oil
1 medium-size onion, chopped
1¼ teaspoons ground cinnamon (or more to taste)
½ teaspoon ground cloves
½ teaspoon ground allspice
¼ teaspoon freshly grated nutmeg
½ medium-size head of red cabbage, shredded (about 7 cups)
6¼ cups water
¼ cup raisins
2 teaspoons mild-flavored honey, such as clover or acacia
salt to taste
2 tart apples, cored and sliced
freshly ground pepper to taste
2 cups plain low-fat yogurt
2 tablespoons fresh lemon juice
1 additional apple, thinly sliced and tossed with lemon juice, for garnish

1. Heat the oil over medium-low heat in a heavy-bottomed soup pot and add the onion. Sauté, stirring, until the onion begins to soften. Add the spices and cook, stirring, for another two to three minutes. Add a tablespoon of water if the spices stick to the bottom of the pot. Add the cabbage and ¼ cup of the water and cook over medium-low heat for five minutes. Add the raisins, honey, water, and salt. Bring to a boil, reduce the heat, cover, and simmer for 30 minutes. **2.** Add the two sliced apples, cover and continue to simmer for another 20 minutes. Add lots of freshly ground pepper, taste, and adjust the seasonings, adding more salt or spices to taste.

3. Remove from the heat and stir in one cup of the yogurt and the lemon juice. Serve at once, topping each bowl with a generous dollop of yogurt and a few apple slices.

Buckwheat Noodle Soup with Tofu, Wild Mushrooms, and Peas

Serves 6

The broth here is downright meaty, and the luxurious porcini make a wonderful match with the earthy buckwheat noodles and humble tofu. Peas add sweetness and color, ginger and cilantro add pungency and zip, and the whole mix is irresistible—and *easy*.

1 ounce (1 cup) dried porcini (cèpes)
2 cups boiling water
1 quart vegetable stock (page 53), garlic broth (page 55), or quick tamari-bouillon (page 54)
2 tablespoons tamari or Kikkoman soy sauce (omit if using quick tamari-bouillon)
1 to 2 teaspoons chopped or grated fresh ginger to taste
6 ounces buckwheat noodles (soba), broken
½ pound firm tofu, cut into small dice
1½ cups fresh (1½ pounds unshelled) or frozen peas
salt and freshly ground pepper to taste
6 tablespoons chopped cilantro for garnish

1. Place the dried mushrooms in a bowl and pour on the boiling water. Let sit for 15 minutes. Strain through a cheesecloth, reserving the soaking liquid. Squeeze the mushrooms over the strainer to extract all of the liquid. Rinse the mushrooms thoroughly in several changes of water and squeeze dry over the strainer. Pour the soaking water into a one quart measure and add enough water to measure three cups.

2. Combine the mushrooms, their soaking liquid, the stock, soy sauce, and ginger in a large soup pot and bring to a boil. Add the noodles, tofu, peas, and salt and pepper. Simmer until the noodles are cooked al dente (about five minutes), adjust the seasonings, and serve, topping each serving with chopped cilantro.

AROMATIC VEGETABLES

These include onions, leeks, carrots, celery, garlic, sometimes fennel, and mushrooms. Onions, leeks, carrots, celery, and garlic are often sautéed in oil or butter before the liquid and remaining ingredients are added, but this isn't always necessary. The vegetables add sweetness and fragrance to a broth as the soup simmers along. Often aromatic vegetables, such as onions, leeks, or carrots, are the main ingredient of a soup.

Corn and Red Pepper Chowder with Fresh Sage

Serves 6

Corn, sweet red peppers, and fresh sage make a stunning combination. The sage and goat cheese add knockout flavors to this elegant chowder.

2 tablespoons olive oil
1 medium-size onion, chopped
2 medium-size red bell peppers, chopped
1 or 2 garlic cloves to taste, minced or put through a press
1½ pounds sweet corn kernels (5 cups, from 5 to 6 ears), fresh or thawed frozen
1 pound (4 medium-size) new or russet potatoes, scrubbed and diced
5 cups vegetable stock (page 53), garlic broth (page 55), or water
salt and freshly ground pepper to taste
½ teaspoon dried thyme *or* 1 teaspoon fresh leaves
2½ cups low-fat milk
3 ounces not-too-salty fresh goat cheese
2 tablespoons slivered fresh sage leaves

1. Heat one tablespoon of the oil over medium-low heat in a heavy-bottomed soup pot and add the onion, one red pepper, and one garlic clove. Sauté, stirring, until tender.
2. Add the remaining garlic if desired, the corn kernels, potatoes, stock or water, salt and pepper, and thyme. →

Bring to a boil, reduce the heat, cover, and simmer for 35 minutes. Meanwhile, sauté the other red pepper in the remaining tablespoon of oil in a small skillet over medium heat until tender. Set aside.

3. Puree half the soup coarsely in a blender or food processor and stir back into the pot along with the milk, sautéed pepper, and more salt and pepper to taste. Heat through without boiling for about 10 minutes. Stir in the cheese and sage, heat through just to melt the cheese, correct the seasonings, and serve.

Garlic Soup with Fusilli and Broccoli

Serves 4

Garlic soups are savory, and they're always comforting and satisfying. This good-looking soup can be thrown together very quickly.

7 cups water
1 bay leaf
1 teaspoon salt or to taste
6 garlic cloves, minced or put through a press
¼ to ½ teaspoon dried thyme, or ½ to 1
    teaspoon fresh leaves to taste
2 teaspoons olive oil
¼ pound (about 1½ cups) fusilli
1 pound (1 medium bunch) broccoli, broken
    into florets
freshly ground pepper to taste
2 medium-size eggs, beaten
¼ cup freshly grated Parmesan or
    Gruyère cheese
2 or 3 tablespoons chopped fresh parsley
    to taste
garlic croutons for garnish (page 58;
    optional)

1. Combine the water, bay leaf, and salt in a soup pot and bring to a simmer. Add the garlic, thyme, and olive oil, cover, and simmer for 15 minutes. Add the fusilli and broccoli, turn up the heat slightly, and continue to simmer, un-→

covered, until the fusilli is cooked al dente, about 10 minutes. Add pepper and adjust the salt.

2. Beat the eggs in a bowl and stir in the cheese and parsley. Ladle some soup into the eggs and stir together. Turn off the heat under the soup and stir the egg mixture into the soup pot. Stir for a minute and serve, garnishing each bowl with croutons if desired.

Note: If you want the broccoli to be crisper, add it to the soup five minutes after the fusilli.

FREEZING SOUPS

SOUPS THAT FREEZE WELL

- Bean soups
- Hearty vegetable soups
- Cooked pureed vegetable soups (*However*, soups containing pureed potatoes need to be reblended and reheated after thawing to reamalgamate the potato starch into the soup. Don't be alarmed by the initial texture after thawing. Reblend, then heat through, stirring with a whisk.)

SOUPS THAT DON'T FREEZE WELL

- Uncooked fruit and vegetable soups
- Garlic soups with lightly cooked green vegetables
- Soups containing tofu
- Noodle soups (*However*, soups containing a relatively small amount of noodles freeze fine. If you want to make a soup that contains noodles for the freezer, omit the noodles and add them when you thaw and reheat the soup.)

HeaRTy Eggplant Soup

This pungent soup is like liquid *baba ghanouj*. It's best if you make it the day before serving. It can be served hot or cold.

3 pounds (3 large) eggplant, cut in half
  lengthwise
5 cups water, garlic broth (page 55), or
  vegetable stock (page 53)
4 large garlic cloves, minced or put through
  a press
½ pound (2 medium-size) new or russet
  potatoes, peeled and diced
1 teaspoon ground cumin
salt to taste
2 to 4 tablespoons fresh lemon juice to taste
1½ cups plain low-fat yogurt
freshly ground pepper to taste
1 large red bell pepper, roasted (can be
  roasted with the eggplant), peeled,
  seeded, and chopped, for garnish
¼ cup chopped fresh cilantro (or more to taste)

1. Preheat the oven to 475 degrees. Score eggplants on the cut side, down to the skin but not through it. Place cut side down on a lightly oiled baking sheet and bake for 30 minutes, until the skins are shriveled and the eggplants are cooked through. Remove from the heat. Allow to cool slightly, then peel and dice.

2. Combine the eggplant, water or stock, three garlic cloves, the potatoes, cumin, and salt in a soup pot and →

bring to a simmer. Cover and simmer for 30 minutes.

3. Puree in a blender or through the medium blade of a food mill and return to the pot. Stir in the lemon juice and the last clove of garlic and heat through. Turn off the heat and whisk in one cup of the yogurt. Add freshly ground pepper and adjust the salt.

4. Serve the soup in warm soup bowls garnished with a dollop of yogurt, a spoonful of the chopped roasted pepper and a sprinkling of cilantro. Or chill and serve cold.

COOKING TIMES

Whereas meat-based soups often require long cooking times and elaborate skimming of fat, vegetable soups can be very quick.

• Soups with hard vegetables like potatoes, carrots, turnips, and winter squash need to simmer from 30 to 45 minutes.

• Bean soups need 45 minutes (for lentils, split peas, and black-eyed peas, none of which requires soaking) to 2 hours.

• Simmer green vegetables for 10 to 15 minutes at most.

Don't cook the life and color out of them. If you're making a large quantity of soup or you're making soup for the freezer, steam the green vegetables separately and stir them into the soup to heat them through shortly before serving.

• Fresh herbs should be added at the very last minute, for maximum flavor and color.

• Add dairy products and eggs at the end of cooking and do not boil, or they will curdle.

Cold Soups

Glistening Summer Borscht

You don't have to be a beet enthusiast to love this enticing, burgundy-hued soup. Infused with garlic, enriched with yogurt or *fromage blanc*, it's sweet and thirst-quenching.

2 pounds beets, peeled and thinly sliced
7 cups water
1 teaspoon salt or to taste
juice of 3 large lemons
1 tablespoon sugar or mild-flavored honey,
   such as clover or acacia
2 garlic cloves, cut in half lengthwise
1½ cups plain low-fat yogurt or *fromage
   blanc* (page 58)
1 small cucumber, peeled, seeded, and
   minced, for garnish
chopped fresh parsley or dill for garnish

1. Combine the beets, water, and a pinch of salt in a soup pot and bring to a simmer. Cover and simmer 30 minutes.

2. Add the lemon juice and continue to simmer, uncovered, for 10 minutes.

3. Add the remaining salt and the sugar or honey and simmer for another 15 minutes. Remove from the heat and add the garlic. Allow to cool, then cover, and chill. Remove the garlic cloves before serving.

4. Ladle the soup into chilled soup bowls. Place about ¼ cup of yogurt or *fromage blanc* in the center of each bowl and top with chopped cucumber and parsley or dill. Serve with black bread or pumpernickel.

Emerald Summer Vegetable Soup

This very refined bright green puree is smooth, just thick enough, and bursting with the sweet flavors of fresh spring and summer vegetables. The herbed whipped cream is a rich finishing touch.

    1 medium-size onion, chopped
    2 leeks, white part only, cleaned and sliced
    1 pound (4 medium-size) new or russet
        potatoes, peeled and diced
    2 large garlic cloves (preferably new spring
        garlic), coarsely chopped
    1 cup shelled fresh or thawed frozen peas
    6 cups vegetable stock (page 53), garlic
        broth (page 55), or water
    salt to taste
    a bouquet garni (page 26)
    1 head of Boston lettuce, washed and
        chopped, *or* ½ pound spinach, stems
        removed and leaves washed
    3 ounces fresh sorrel, washed and
        stems removed
    1 bunch of fresh parsley, stems removed
    freshly ground pepper to taste
    1 cup plain low-fat yogurt
    6 tablespoons herbed whipped cream
        (page 60) for garnish
    fresh parsley, tarragon, chervil, or basil
        sprigs for garnish

1. Combine the onions, leeks, potatoes, garlic, peas, stock or water, salt if necessary, and bouquet garni in a large soup pot; bring to a boil. Reduce the heat and simmer for 30 minutes. Add the lettuce or spinach and half the sorrel and simmer for another five to eight minutes (the sorrel will lose its bright color, but the lettuce or spinach should stay bright green). Add the parsley and remaining sorrel and remove from the heat. Puree in a blender or food processor in batches until completely smooth. Taste for salt and pepper and transfer to a bowl. Allow to cool, then chill for a few hours. Whisk in the yogurt.

2. Spoon the soup into chilled bowls, top each serving with a tablespoon of the herbed whipped cream, garnish with a sprig or two of herbs, and serve.

Note: The soup is also good hot.

Chilled Cherry-Yogurt Soup

Serves 4

This gorgeous, sweet, and lemony soup makes a great late spring/early summer light lunch or supper.

2¾ pounds ripe Bing or black cherries
3 cups water
zest of 2 large lemons
2 tablespoons sugar
10 tablespoons fresh lemon juice
4 teaspoons kirsch
2 cups plain low-fat yogurt
fresh mint leaves or sprigs for garnish

1. Set aside 12 to 16 cherries for garnish. Pit the rest over a bowl and retain the pits.
2. Combine the pits and one cup of the water in a small saucepan. Combine the pitted cherries, the remaining two cups water, the lemon zest, and the sugar in a large saucepan. Bring both saucepans to a boil, reduce the heat, and simmer, uncovered, for five minutes. Remove from the heat. Strain the water from the pits into the cherries. Discard pits.
3. Blend the contents of the saucepan in a blender until smooth. Transfer to a bowl and stir in ½ cup of the lemon juice and the kirsch. Allow to cool and refrigerate.
4. When the mixture is chilled, whisk in the yogurt and remaining lemon juice. Serve, garnishing each bowl with a few whole cherries and a sprig or a few leaves of mint.

46

Potato-Leek Soup with Chervil

Serves 6

The cold version of this creamy, refreshing soup is the familiar *vichyssoise*. The traditional French soup calls for cream, but I use yogurt or *fromage blanc*, which makes a tarter version. Chives are the traditional garnish, but try it with chervil, which has a more interesting flavor.

3 medium-size leeks, white part only,
   cleaned and sliced
1½ pounds (6 medium-size) new or russet
   potatoes, peeled and diced
5 cups water or vegetable stock (page 53)
a bouquet garni (page 26)
salt to taste
1½ cups low-fat milk
freshly ground pepper to taste
1 cup plain low-fat yogurt or *fromage blanc*
   (page 58), *or* 2½ cups milk in all
6 tablespoons chopped fresh chervil or chives

1. Combine the leeks, potatoes, water or stock, bouquet garni, and salt in a soup pot. Bring to a boil, reduce the heat, cover, and simmer for 45 minutes. Remove the bouquet garni.

2. Puree the soup in a blender or through the fine or medium blade of a food mill. Return to the pot and stir in the milk and lots of pepper. Heat through, stirring, and adjust the seasonings. If you're serving the soup hot, whisk in the→

yogurt or *fromage blanc* off the heat and serve, topping each bowl with a tablespoon of fresh chervil.

3. If you're serving it cold, cool and chill before whisking in the yogurt or *fromage blanc*. Stir it in just before serving, adjust the seasonings, and serve, topping each bowl with chopped fresh chervil or chives.

Tangy Cream of Sorrel Soup

This tangy soup can be served hot or cold. You might want a slightly thicker soup if you're serving it hot, in which case use the smaller amount of milk.

½ pound sorrel, stems removed and washed
  (5 cups leaves)
4 teaspoons olive oil, sunflower oil, or
  unsalted butter
1 medium-size onion, chopped
2 garlic cloves, minced or put through a press
1¼ pounds (5 medium-size) new or russet
  potatoes, peeled and chopped
1 quart vegetable stock (page 53), garlic
  broth (page 55) or water
1 bay leaf
salt to taste
1 to 1½ cups low-fat milk to taste
freshly ground pepper to taste
1 cup plain low-fat yogurt (or more to taste)

1. Set aside a couple of sorrel leaves and cut into thin slivers for garnish.

2. Heat the oil or butter over low heat in a heavy-bottomed soup pot and add the onion and one garlic clove. Partially cover and cook, stirring often, for five to 10 minutes, until the onion is soft and fragrant. Do not brown.

3. Add the remaining garlic, the potatoes, stock or water, bay leaf, and salt and bring to a boil. Reduce the heat, cover, and simmer for 30 minutes or until the potatoes are tender. Remove the bay leaf. Add the sorrel and simmer for another 10 minutes.

4. Puree in a blender or through a food mill and return to the pot. Stir in the milk and pepper and heat through. Taste and adjust the salt.

5. Serve hot or cold, garnishing each bowl with a generous dollop of yogurt and a sprinkling of slivered sorrel.

Cold Tomato Soup with Olivada Garnish

Come summertime, I could live on this light, tomatoey soup. It's much like a blender gazpacho, cooling and envigorating. The olivada garnish gives the dish a Provençal twist.

2½ pounds (10 medium-size) ripe tomatoes, peeled and quartered

½ long European cucumber *or* 1 small ordinary cucumber, peeled, seeded, and cut into chunks

1 large carrot, cut into chunks

1 medium-size red or white onion, quartered

2 large garlic cloves

5 tablespoons fresh lemon juice

2 tablespoons red wine vinegar

1 tablespoon olive oil

½ teaspoon Worcestershire sauce

2 tablespoons tightly packed fresh basil leaves

1½ cups water

salt (about 1 heaped teaspoon) and freshly ground pepper to taste

½ cup *fromage blanc* (page 58) or plain low-fat yogurt for garnish

¼ pound firm tofu, cut into small cubes and sprinkled with tamari or Kikkoman soy sauce (optional)

4 teaspoons olivada (page 61)

4 attractive fresh basil sprigs for garnish

1. In a blender, puree the vegetables and garlic in batches with the lemon juice, vinegar, olive oil, Worcestershire sauce, basil leaves, water, and salt and pepper until smooth. Strain into a bowl through a medium strainer, using the back of a spoon to push all the soup through. Taste and adjust seasonings. Cover and refrigerate until serving.

2. Chill four soup bowls. Place an ice cube in each bowl if you wish and ladle in the soup. Place two tablespoons of *fromage blanc* or yogurt in the middle of each serving and top with cubed tofu if desired and a teaspoon of olivada and a basil sprig. Serve at once.

Stocks and Garnishes

Stocks

Vegetable-based stocks have one clear advantage over meat stocks: they are extremely quick to make and require no skimming of fat. Each of these is distinctive: the vegetable stock is mild and fragrant, the garlic stock full-bodied but not pungent (a good substitute for chicken stock), the mushroom broth "meaty"-flavored with great depth, and the ginger stock spicy. For an instant savory vegetarian stock, try the Quick Tamari-Bouillon.

Vegetable Stock

Makes 7 cups

2 quarts water
2 large onions, quartered
2 large carrots, coarsely sliced
2 large leeks, cleaned and sliced
3 garlic cloves, peeled
2 celery ribs, with leaves, coarsely sliced
a bouquet garni (page 26)
½ pound (2 medium-size) new or russet
   potatoes, scrubbed and diced
salt to taste
1 teaspoon peppercorns

1. Combine all the ingredients in a stockpot and bring to a boil. Reduce the heat, cover, and simmer for one to two hours. Strain and discard the vegetables. This will keep for four days in the refrigerator and freezes well.

Ginger-Vegetable Stock

This is great for spicy Asian soups. To the ingredients for the preceding vegetable stock, add a 2-inch piece of fresh ginger, peeled and sliced or chopped, and 2 tablespoons tamari or Kikkoman soy sauce. Proceed as directed.

Quick Tamari-Bouillon

The tamari gives this instant stock an Asian flavor. It's essential that you get good-quality bouillon cubes for this, or the stock will have a metallic, chemical flavor. You can find unadulterated vegetable bouillon cubes in whole foods stores.

    1 quart water
    2 vegetable bouillon cubes
    2 to 3 tablespoons tamari or Kikkoman soy
        sauce to taste

1. Bring the water to a boil and dissolve the bouillon cubes in it. Add the soy sauce and use as a stock for soups.

Garlic Broth

Even though there are two heads of garlic here, this stock is fragrant rather than pungent. Its reputation as a remedy in my house equals that of chicken soup.

> 2 quarts water
> 2 heads of garlic, cloves separated and
>   peeled (see note)
> a bouquet garni (page 26)
> ½ teaspoon dried thyme
> 1 to 2 teaspoons salt to taste
> 6 peppercorns
> 1 tablespoon olive oil

1. Combine all the ingredients in a stockpot and bring to a boil. Cover, reduce the heat, and simmer for 1 to 2 hours. Strain and adjust the salt. This will keep for three or four days in the refrigerator and freezes well.

Note: To peel all the garlic cloves, hit them with the bottom of a jar or glass or lean on them with the flat side of a knife. The skins will pop off, and it doesn't matter if the garlic cloves are slightly crushed.

INTeNSe MushRooM BRoTh

This broth, which is nothing more than the soaking water from dried porcini, is positively meaty. I use it for minestrone and other hearty vegetable soups, as well as some Asian broths. Don't throw away the mushrooms; use them in stir-fries, quiches, soups, and salads. The broth keeps for two days in the refrigerator and can be frozen.

2 ounces (2 cups) dried porcini (cèpes)
1 quart boiling water
salt and freshly ground pepper to taste
1 tablespoon tamari or Kikkoman soy sauce
   (optional)

1. Place the mushrooms in a bowl and pour on the boiling water. Let sit for 30 minutes. Drain the soaking water through a cheesecloth-lined strainer into a bowl. Squeeze the mushrooms over the strainer to extract all the liquid. Add more water to the soaking liquid to make six cups (or one quart for a stronger broth). Season to taste with salt, pepper, and soy sauce if desired.

2. Rinse the mushrooms thoroughly in several changes of water, squeeze dry, and keep for another use.

Soup Garnishes

Garnishes should do more than just decorate; they should add a final bit of unexpected flavor and texture (be it creaminess or crunch). They have the power to transform something familiar into an utterly original dish. Sometimes it's the flavor of a lively herb, like mint or cilantro, that really brings the soup to life. Even something as simple as a garlic crouton can introduce a certain element that is necessary if the soup is really going to be memorable. Garnishes like yogurt, *fromage blanc*, and grated Parmesan or Gruyère cheese can also provide a meatless soup with an extra hit of protein.

The color element is quite important for those soups that are not inherently bright, like the Hearty Eggplant Soup on page 39, the Black-Eyed Pea Soup with Cilantro and Cumin (page 20), or the Brazilian Black Bean Soup on page 17. These soups taste delicious, but they need some visual dazzle, and bright red roasted peppers or emerald green herbs will provide it.

Here are the garnishes I use most often:

Garlic croutons*
Roasted red peppers
Fromage blanc*
Olivada*
Herbed whipped cream*
Chopped fresh herbs, especially parsley, cilantro, chives, chervil, basil, dill, and mint
Plain low-fat yogurt
Freshly grated Parmesan cheese
Freshly grated Gruyère cheese
Alfalfa sprouts (very good with cold vegetable soups)
Sunflower seeds
Toasted pine nuts
Diced or minced vegetables
Thin slices of lemon or lime

*Recipe follows

GaRLic CRouToNS

1. Begin with a good loaf of French bread or whole wheat country bread, not floppy or crumbly bread. Toast thin slices in a toaster or in the oven until crisp. Remove from the heat and rub with a halved clove of garlic.

2. If you wish, brush lightly with olive oil. Cut into small dice (leave baguette slices as they are), and cut irregular-shaped loaves into baguette-size (1- to 1½-inch) pieces. Croutons will keep for a day or so, wrapped in foil.

FRomage BLaNc

Makes 1 cup

Fromage blanc is a fermented milk product, somewhat like a cross between cottage cheese and yogurt. It comes in very low-fat versions. I prefer it to yogurt for dolloping onto soups because it's creamier and less acidic. You can make something that resembles *fromage blanc* by blending cottage cheese and plain low-fat yogurt together until smooth. You can find *fromage blanc* in some gourmet stores.

¾ cup sieved low-fat cottage cheese
¼ cup plain low-fat yogurt

1. Blend together the cottage cheese and yogurt in a food processor until completely smooth. Transfer to a covered container and refrigerate.

HeRbed FRoMage BLanc
oR YoguRT

Here is a lower-fat, more acidic version. Substitute plain low-fat yogurt or *fromage blanc* (page 58) for the cream (you will need about ⅔ cup to make the same amount). Stir together with the herbs used for herbed whipped cream (page 60) and proceed as directed.

HeRBed Whipped CReaM

Some of this sublime whipped cream remains stiff; some of it melts into the surface of the soup. It's especially good with pureed soups. Use a mix of delicate herbs such as those listed below.

½ cup whipping cream
6 tablespoons finely chopped fresh herbs
such as tarragon, chervil, basil, parsley,
or chives

1. Whip the cream until fairly stiff. Stir in the herbs. Spoon a tablespoon onto each bowl of soup just before serving.

ROASTED RED BELL PEPPERS

There are several ways to roast the peppers. You can place them directly in a gas flame or below a broiler. Or you can place them in a dry skillet over an electric or gas burner or in a baking dish in a 450-degree oven. You want all the skin to blister and blacken. Keep turning the peppers until they are uniformly charred, then place them in a plastic bag or a tightly covered bowl until cool enough to handle.

Peel off the blackened skin, split in half over a bowl (to retain the juice), and remove and discard the seeds and inner membranes. Rinse quickly under cool water and pat dry. Cut the halved peppers in half lengthwise, then into thin strips or small dice. Place in a bowl or serving dish and toss with a few tablespoons of olive oil, some minced garlic if you wish, and salt to taste. Cover and refrigerate. The peppers will keep for 5 days in the refrigerator.

Olivada

Olive paste is called *tapenade* when it contains capers; Provençal tapenade is a complex mixture made from olives, capers, anchovies, garlic, and herbs. This is a simpler puree, meant to be used as a spread for croutons and a delicious garnish for soups.

½ pound imported black Provençal or
   Greek olives, pitted
2 garlic cloves, minced or put through a press
¼ to ½ teaspoon dried thyme *or* ½ to 1
   teaspoon fresh leaves to taste
¼ to ½ teaspoon crushed dried rosemary *or*
   ½ to 1 teaspoon chopped fresh to taste
2 tablespoons fresh lemon juice
1 teaspoon Dijon mustard (optional)
2 tablespoons olive oil
lots of freshly ground black pepper

1. Puree the olives and remaining ingredients in a mortar and pestle or in a food processor. When you have achieved a smooth paste, transfer it to a bowl, cover, and refrigerate until ready to use.

2. To use as a garnish for soups, spread on garlic croutons and top the soup with the croutons or place dollops directly on each serving of soup.

METRIC CONVERSION CHART

CONVERSIONS OF OUNCES TO GRAMS

Ounces (oz)	Grams (g)
1 oz	30 g*
2 oz	60 g
3 oz	85 g
4 oz	115 g
5 oz	140 g
6 oz	180 g
7 oz	200 g
8 oz	225 g
9 oz	250 g
10 oz	285 g
11 oz	300 g
12 oz	340 g
13 oz	370 g
14 oz	400 g
15 oz	425 g
16 oz	450 g
20 oz	570 g
24 oz	680 g
28 oz	790 g
32 oz	900 g

*Approximate. To convert ounces to grams, multiply number of ounces by 28.35.

CONVERSIONS OF FAHRENHEIT TO CELSIUS

Fahrenheit	Celsius
170°F	77°C*
180°F	82°C
190°F	88°C
200°F	95°C
225°F	110°C
250°F	120°C
300°F	150°C
325°F	165°C
350°F	180°C
375°F	190°C
400°F	205°C
425°F	220°C
450°F	230°C
475°F	245°C
500°F	260°C
525°F	275°C
550°F	290°C

*Approximate. To convert Fahrenheit to Celsius, subtract 32, multiply by 5, then divide by 9.

CONVERSIONS OF POUNDS TO GRAMS AND KILOGRAMS

Pounds (lb)	Grams (g); kilograms (kg)
1 lb	450 g*
1¼ lb	565 g
1½ lb	675 g
1¾ lb	800 g
2 lb	900 g
2½ lb	1,125 g; 1¼ kg
3 lb	1,350 g
3½ lb	1,500 g; 1½ kg
4 lb	1,800 g
4½ lb	2 kg
5 lb	2¼ kg
5½ lb	2½ kg
6 lb	2¾ kg
6½ lb	3 kg
7 lb	3¼ kg
7½ lb	3½ kg
8 lb	3¾ kg
9 lb	4 kg
10 lb	4½ kg

*Approximate. To convert pounds into kilograms, multiply number of pounds by 453.6.

CONVERSIONS OF QUARTS TO LITERS

Quarts (qt)	Liters (L)
1 qt	1 L*
1½ qt	1½ L
2 qt	2 L
2½ qt	2½ L
3 qt	2¾ L
4 qt	3¾ L
5 qt	4¾ L
6 qt	5½ L
7 qt	6½ L
8 qt	7½ L
9 qt	8½ L
10 qt	9½ L

*Approximate. To convert quarts to liters, multiply number of quarts by 0.95.